Love God, Live Life
7 Principles for a Victorious Christian Life in a Busy World

By
Sarah Gabrielson

Copyright © 2011 by Sarah Gabrielson

Love God, Live Life
7 Principles for a Victorious Christian Life in a Busy World
by Sarah Gabrielson

Printed in the United States of America

ISBN 9781613797044

All rights reserved solely by the author. The author guarantees all contents are original and do not infringe upon the legal rights of any other person or work. No part of this book may be reproduced in any form without the permission of the author. The views expressed in this book are not necessarily those of the publisher.

Unless otherwise indicated, Bible quotations are taken from The NKJV of the Bible. Copyright © 1982 by Thomas Nelson Inc.; and The American Standard Version of the Bible.

www.xulonpress.com

Dedication

First of all I would like to thank God. This was His idea and I couldn't have done it without Him. I would like to dedicate this book to all of the wonderful friends and family who offered countless hours of prayer support and endless encouragement. Thanks to my parents who have raised me up in the way I should go. Thank you to my sisters in Christ who prayed for me at the promptings of the Spirit no matter what time of night or day. Thanks to my husband for his endless support, and to my children, Hannah, Sophia and Michael for being patient while Mommy was working. Thanks to Gayla for your technical help. Thanks to Pastor Tim and Teresa for their spiritual guidance throughout the past ten years. Thanks to Pastor Brian and Shelly at Joy Christian Center, Pastor Doug and Peggy at The Waters, and Pastor John and Shannon at Northstar, for all you have done for me and all you do for the Body of Christ. Each and every one of you has played a special and unique role in the writing of this book. I love and appreciate all of you. Thank you.

Contents

Introduction ix
Chapter 1 The Most Important Step 11
Chapter 2 The Power and the
    Door – The Holy Spirit 17
Chapter 3 The Word 33
Chapter 4 The Importance of Worship ... 45
Chapter 5 Offense and Bitterness –
    The Victory Blockers 55
Chapter 6 Prayer and Fasting – A Key
    to Overcome 65
Chapter 7 Spiritual Warfare 73
Chapter 8 Putting it Together – A
    Victorious Life 83

Introduction

I am a mom. I'm a mom on a mission to balance a victorious life for Christ and the busy everyday duties that are part of this life.

Let's face it. We live in a busy time. We are expected to juggle so much, as parents or just as people. How do we fit God into the equation, but not only fit Him in, put Him first? And when He is first, how do we really live victorious and not just get by?

As part of my mission, I have read many books and spent countless hours praying and listening to the promptings of the Holy Spirit. I found that many of the things I read and teachings I heard had great wisdom but did not seem possible in my current season of life. I found myself praying for ways to work around my responsibilities as a busy mother of three small children.

This book is a compilation of some of the revelations I've had. I don't believe there is a model or formula that applies to every person, but there are some very specific steps that can be taken to help you find a place where you can pray, hear and come to a place of victory in your life. Jesus says in John 16:33, "...in Me you may have peace. In the world you will have tribulation; but be of good cheer, I have overcome the world."

Chapter 1

The Most Important Step

that if you confess with your mouth the Lord Jesus and believe in your heart that God has raised Him from the dead, you will be saved. For with the heart one believes unto righteousness, and with the mouth confession is made unto salvation. (Romans 10: 9, 10)

The first principle to living a victorious life for Christ is to become "born again". Jesus mentions it in the Bible when he is talking to Nicodemus, a ruler of the Jewish people, recorded in John 3. Jesus answered and said to him, "most assuredly, I say to you, unless one is born again, he cannot enter the kingdom of God." (John 3:3)

Guess what? Becoming born again is the easiest and the fastest thing you can do to begin a relationship with the God who has made you and Christ who came as a man and died for your sins. What does it mean, exactly, to be born again? Spiritually, it means that you have passed from darkness to light. You have moved from having a dead spirit living inside you to a brand new clean spirit. You are forgiven of your sins and made completely new in the eyes of your Savior who loves you. An amazing transformation happens inside you. The Bible says, "Therefore, if anyone is in Christ, he is a new creation; old things have passed away; behold all things have become new." (2 Corinthians 5:17). It's like a child with no home, no bed, no one to love her, being adopted into the richest family in the world. She doesn't have anything to offer, but suddenly she has a relationship with a father. Not a father who hires a nanny to take care of her, but one who loves her and personally takes care of her every need.

Becoming born again is the first work that the Holy Spirit does in the believer's life. It is a major miracle, and one of the most important miracles that happens to any person. Once a person is born again, they will go to heaven not hell. We are

Love God, Live Life

all eternal beings. That means that even though our body may die our spirit lives on forever. There are only two places our spirit can reside, in peace with Christ for eternity or in hell.

People have different "methods" of becoming born again. Some might say a particular prayer. Others will have you recite scripture. Some might ask you to come forward in an assembly of some type like a church service. I believe that the method is not as important as the heart behind it. Someone may go through all the planned sequence of events. They close their eyes and raise their hands. They go forward and say the prayer. However, if there is not surrender in their heart, a desire to give it all to God, they are not different than when they started. Another person however, may skip all those steps and say a simple prayer in their car on the way home and become born again. The difference is realizing and accepting the reality of Christ. It is believing that reality and confessing it even when the little thoughts come into your head from the enemy, telling you you're not born again. Satan and his army of demons do exist, and their mission in this life is to confuse you and create any divisions they can to keep you from the truth and from a relationship with your Savior.

This is an important thing to remember with each of the principles outlined in this book. There is not a specific formula for everyone. Becoming born again is just about understanding you were a sinner and now because of the sacrifice of Jesus, the Son of the one true God, you are forgiven. You are a changed person. You need to believe it. There are certain things you can do that can make this seem more real to you, but you need to believe it first to get to those things.

Becoming born again is the easiest and fastest step to a victorious life for God and really a victorious life in this world. Once you realize the fullness of this, you can believe for any promise in the Bible because it is yours. For example, you can believe for divine health. The prophet Isaiah spoke of this before Jesus was even born when he said, "But He was wounded for our transgressions, He was bruised for our iniquities; The chastisement for our peace was upon Him, And by His stripes we are healed." (Isaiah 53:5)

Peter, a man who lived with Jesus and experienced his life, death and resurrection first hand, reminds us of it again, "who Himself bore our sins in His own body on the tree, that we, having died to sins, might live for righteousness—by whose stripes you were healed." (1 Peter 2:24). This means that the suffering of Christ on the cross, made way for us to live in health. As the men were beating Jesus and slashing him (the stripes are bruises and wounds from this act), we were being made whole. Not only were our sins taken from us, but our bodies were made well. That means it's already been done. We have already been healed. Do you feel sick today? Ask God to heal you and believe it's already happened.

Does this mean a born again believer will never get sick? It is possible, if a person can build their faith to the point that they will believe they are healthy and whole no matter how they feel that day. Once you are born again you need to believe that God has removed your old sinful man from you and replaced it with a fresh new one. You need to believe you are alive in Christ and not let Satan convince you that you are still dead in him.

Once you are born again, you can believe you are no longer in poverty, that you have more than enough, that God will provide for your every need. He wants to provide for us, He has promised it in His Word. There are important steps to working in the economy of God, and you could read an entire book on the subject. There are many good things out there to help you learn and grow. Start at the beginning by believing.

Are you ready? Now is the time to take the first step.

> Father, I call on you in the name of Jesus. I ask you to be Lord of my life from this day forward. I do as Romans 8 tells me in your Holy Word. I say, Jesus, you are Lord. Lord of my life. I believe that you died on the cross and shed blood as a perfect sacrifice for my sins. Cleanse me from these sins. I am sorry. Please forgive me. Thank you, Holy Spirit, for making me a new creation. I believe these things in my heart, and today is a new day because of you Jesus. Amen.

You are on your way to victory. Believe it and know it. Today is the day to begin your new day. It's the first day of many great days to come.

Chapter 2

The Power and the Door - The Holy Spirit

Now may the God of hope fill you with all joy and peace in believing, that you may abound in hope by the power of the Holy Spirit.(Romans 15:13)

Another principle of living a victorious life for Christ, is getting to know the person of the Holy Spirit. That's right, the person. He is the Spirit of God, and He is a person. Many people think of the Holy Spirit as some sort of overriding force, or a wind that comes. He's that too, but to really learn and grow in the Holy Spirit it is important for us to see Him as a person. We are spirit, soul and body. We have three parts to our whole person. We wouldn't consider our spirit different than the rest of our body. It is not less of our person. The Holy Spirit is the Spirit of God and is the person of God. He was present when the Creator of the universe made you. He listened to the plan for your life, and He knows each and every detail that our Father has for you in this life. The really awesome thing is that He can live inside you and reveal that plan to you as you go through this life. He also can help your spirit to pray out that perfect plan for your life.

The topic of the Holy Spirit is a controversial one. There is much confusion and division in churches about it. Confusion and division is not from God. It is actually contrary to His very nature. They are ploys by the enemy, by Satan, to keep you from taking a step that will move you into a victorious life. Do not let him do it. My goal is to share what I believe is the truth on the subject. People will say that the Holy Spirit is not for today. People will say that they believe in the Holy Trinity, the Father, Son and Holy Spirit and confess it as their faith and then ignore the wonderful gift that God has given them by having His Spirit available to you as a helper, a guide and a prayer warrior.

The Holy Spirit is mentioned many times in the Word of God in the Old and New Testament. There are entire chapters that describe Him and His works and the spiritual gifts that can come and work because of Him. Many names are used to describe the Holy Spirit, and in no place does it say specifically and in context to the story that the Holy Spirit is not for today. The Word says in Hebrews 13:8 that Jesus Christ is the same yesterday, today and forever; and, since God is a three part being, God the Father, God the Son (Jesus) and God the Holy Spirit, we can conclude then that the Holy Spirit is the same yesterday, today and forever. This leaves no room for confusion or division. It is straight forward. The Holy Spirit is alive and working today just as He was in Biblical times. That means the Spiritual Gifts we see outlined in 1 Corinthians 12, word of wisdom, word of knowledge, gift of faith, gifts of healings, working of miracles, prophecy, discerning of spirits, different kinds of tongues, and interpretation of tongues are all available to us today as the Spirit wills.

Have you ever read through the Bible and wondered what you just read? Have you ever been in a situation where you were not sure of the truth, but you really needed to know it? The Holy Spirit is called the Spirit of Truth, and one of His main purposes is to reveal the truth to you. You don't need to wonder anymore, because you can have the God given truth revealed to you, if you seek and accept this gift.

Have you ever needed help in a situation and just didn't know which way to turn? The Holy Spirit is referred to as your Helper. That is another of His main purposes. The Spirit of the Creator of the Universe, who knows the mind of God and His perfect will for your life, can be with you, with answers for every situation or question you have in this life. When you don't know how to pray, He does. When you don't know who to ask or what action to take, He does. He is the direct line to God, and the power to take action on what is revealed.

At the end of Chapter 15 and then Chapter 16 in the book of John, we see Jesus speaking to His disciples. He is telling them that He will be leaving them. He tells them that it is for the best because once He is gone then the Holy Spirit, The Helper, He later calls Him the Spirit of Truth, can come. Now, let's put this in perspective. These were the closest men to Jesus. They had walked with Him through all of His teaching. They witnessed people healed and demons cast out. I know I would have had difficulty believing that the Person/Spirit who would replace Him in my life could be better. I'm sure I would have been asking how it was possible. Well, Jesus was one man, in only one place at a time.

Love God, Live Life

The Holy Spirit is Jesus everywhere all the time. I would say that's better for you and me because we are able to have and witness the same truth, the same teaching, the same help, the same healing, and the same power here and now. He can live and breathe and move with you and through you at all times. This is the reason God can be the same, yesterday, today and forever.

In the Old Testament, we see a number of great men who seemed to have direct connection with God. There were many prophets and kings and great men of God who heard His voice in various ways, like Joseph through his dreams. This was by the power of the Holy Spirit and as the Spirit willed. God would send His Spirit. He would come upon these men for a time or a specific purpose and then He would leave. However, now that Jesus has died for our sins, we can have that direct connect with God at all times; and since Jesus has left this earth, we can have the Holy Spirit living with us and in us each and every day of our lives. It is a gift for all that hunger to have it.

You're probably thinking one of two things at this point. The first might be, "I want that. How do I get it?" The second might be, "I don't want that, I am afraid of it." I will address the first attitude very soon. Do not skip this part because most of us have a certain amount of fear about the Holy Spirit, even if we don't realize it. Unfortunately, at some point in your Christian walk the chances are pretty good that you have encountered someone who has said something like, "this is not something you should be pursuing, it's not Biblical, it is not for today." Maybe you have experienced something yourself that was "weird" or "not right", and you have serious questions about this topic. I understand and I have had similar thoughts about some things I have experienced. I encourage you to look up Holy Spirit in a good concordance and see what the Word says about Him. Many Bibles have a concordance in them at the back. It won't be extensive but it is a place to start. While you're at it, look up some of the other names of the Holy Spirit: Spirit of Truth, Comforter, or Helper. There is a great deal in God's Word on the subject. Pray that revelation will come to you. Ask the Spirit of Truth to reveal truth to you. Keep in mind that fear is not from God. It is contrary to His nature and contrary to faith itself. You cannot be in faith about a situation and be in fear at the same time. It's impossible. The truth is, if you choose to not open your mind to the possibility that this awesome power is available to you today and now, you will not receive it. You can't. The Holy Spirit is a gentleman, and

Love God, Live Life

He will only fill you if you invite Him. Some say, He will only fill you if you hunger for Him. I would say hunger could be described as a strong invite.

If you are in fear about the Holy Spirit, tell that fear to get under your feet. Fear is a work of the enemy, it usually comes as a thought, and it is not from God. Many people mistake fear for their "inner witness". The inner witness can be described as the voice of the Holy Spirit speaking to you to tell you which way to go or what to do in a situation. Some people may call it their conscience. This is very real. Holy Spirit does not cause fear.

We are three part beings, made in the image of God. We have a spirit, a soul and a body. The spirit is what is changed when you become born again, and where the Holy Spirit lives and works and speaks, when you have received the baptism of the Holy Spirit – when we invite Him to fill us. It is a separate place from the body, and the soul. The body is the vehicle. It's what we ride around in on this earth. Our body is an important piece, because our spirit would not have fingers or toes or feet. Without our body, our spirit would not have a tongue to speak and feet to move and be able to go where God would have us go. They work together, but they are different. In a similar way, we have a soul. It's where our thoughts and emotions reside. Something that happens in our spirit may move our emotions. They work together, but they are two different things.

Your inner witness will not sound like emotion. It will sound like a calm do this or don't do that kind of voice. Your inner witness is from your spirit, and so it is separate from emotion. Sometimes our emotions will be moved by something that our inner witness might reveal, but at first, it is without emotion.

There are other hindrances that might keep you from receiving the Holy Spirit, but it seems like fear is one of the things that the enemy uses most often. Fear can take many forms. You can pray and ask for revelation, and God will reveal your fear to you. Don't let it stop you.

As I mentioned previously, you will find the gifts of the Spirit as you look into the Word. One of those gifts is different kinds of tongues. In almost all of the stories in the Bible when people received the baptism of the Holy Spirit, they received The Holy Spirit and then prayed in tongues. Tongues were the outward evidence that they had received Him. We see this in Acts 2:1-4, the day of Pentecost. It says they were filled with the Holy Spirit and began to speak with other tongues. In Acts 10: 44-46, the Holy Spirit poured out on the Gentiles, and

Love God, Live Life

they spoke with tongues. In Acts 19:1-6, Paul laid hands on people and they received the Holy Spirit and spoke with tongues. We see a pattern in the Word of God. Since we are clear that God is the same yesterday, today and forever because the Word of God tells us this, we can then expect that when we are baptized in the Holy Spirit, when we hunger for Him and invite Him to fill us, we will also speak in tongues. Not only should we expect to speak in tongues, we should believe it is the door that allows the Holy Spirit to work through us, as He sees necessary, with all of the other spiritual gifts. In these stories, tongues was the first evidence that someone had been baptized in the Holy Spirit. Will tongues always come first? Different churches have different doctrines on the subject. My belief is that they do. In these cases in the Word they did; and in my life tongues has proven to be a door that opened to many victories, true revelation and miraculous works of God.

There is also some confusion regarding the difference between becoming born again and the baptism of the Holy Spirit. Some argue that they are one in the same, and that when you are born again you have all of the Holy Spirit you can have. Let me be very clear, because the Word of God is clear. If you are born again, you will go to heaven. You do not need to be baptized in the Holy

Spirit to go to heaven. When you are born again, your old spirit is changed into a new creation and is rewired. Your old nature is gone. You can live a fine Christian life. When you are baptized in the Holy Spirit however, the power switch to all that new wiring is turned on. That is, if you charge up the battery. This is where praying in tongues becomes important. It is not exactly like charging up the battery, but it's a good analogy. When we are praying in tongues for spiritual edification, which is usually the first type of tongues that will come out of your mouth, it's like exercise for our spirit. Exercise is important for strengthening your body, and if you do it diligently, you can become a body builder with huge muscles. Praying in tongues is similar, the more you do it, the stronger your spirit will get. Strength is really only the beginning. The power that raised Jesus from the dead can be the same power living and moving in you, if you turn on the switch. This is a key to victory in Christ.

People will tell you different "methods" of being baptized in the Holy Spirit, and again, there is not a specific formula. Some come forward in a meeting and have hands laid on them and receive it. That is a good way, but it doesn't have to happen that way. I received it all by myself in my bedroom. I honestly don't remember all of the circumstances of how He filled me, I think I prayed earlier in the night with someone about it. I do remember clearly however, that it wasn't until I was in my room when I was really able to focus on God and get past my fear that tongues started flowing. I said it once and it's important to not forget that the Holy Spirit is a gentleman, and He will not force Himself in. In fact He won't come unless He knows you are sure. That means you need to invite Him. You need to hunger to have Him come. It is a gift given to us at Pentecost. All we really have to do is receive Him. If you have fear or doubt, it will probably stop you from receiving. If you have opened the door to anything that may be in His spot, you will need to take care of that first. Ask for forgiveness for opening the door, and speak to anything that may have unknowingly taken a place in you. Tell it, it is under your feet. Then, ask the Holy Spirit to come in. Ask Him to fill you up to overflowing. Say, "I expect to speak with other tongues as You give me utterance" (Acts 2:4) and start praising God for your baptism. Just open your mouth and speak anything. You have to cooperate with the Holy Spirit to do this, he provides the prayer but your mouth has to speak it out. Many times the tongues will just come. At first, they may be only a few syllables or sounds. Keep it up. You wouldn't expect a baby to speak out full complete sentences. Your language will grow and change as your spirit grows and changes. Remember, it is the perfect prayer for you at the time. As you speak in tongues, your spirit will get stronger; and the stronger you get the more the power from the Holy Spirit can flow.

Some people do not speak in tongues right away. Often people pray to receive the baptism of the Holy Spirit, receive it, and they just won't use their lips and voice to speak it out. Sometimes they are actually speaking in tongues, but it doesn't sound the way they think it should, so they convince themselves they have not received. Other times, there may be a different hindrance that they are not even aware of. If this happens to you, ask God to reveal it to you. Don't give up. Don't get discouraged. That would be exactly what Satan wants you to do. Satan doesn't want you to have the baptism of the Holy Spirit, and tongues, because it will make you much more of a threat to him. Get really hungry. Don't take no for an answer. In this particular case, no is not an answer from God. He gives this freely to us. Be sure, believe, and say something from a heart of praise. If you're not praying in tongues right away, don't get discouraged and quit reading this book. This is only one principle, and more knowledge can help.

Now you pray in tongues, what's next? Well you should pray in tongues as often as you can. Many teachers on the subject will say an hour a day or more. Don't let that be a road block to you. So many people hear a teaching on something with a specific amount of time, and it trips them up. If you can't seem to think of how, in your busy day, you could possibly pray in tongues an hour a day, let me give you a few options. First of all, any amount of praying in tongues is better than none. You can pray in tongues anytime you want to when you are praying for personal edification. It is as the Spirit wills, but it is the only spiritual gift you have the ability to shut on and off simply by doing it. All the rest, the Holy Spirit shuts on and off. You can pray in tongues as you wake up in the morning, while you're in the shower, while you're doing your hair, or while you're on your way to work. You can pray in tongues in the car, or while your washing dishes. Anytime you have time for a free thought, you have time to pray in tongues.

God isn't hard of hearing either. You don't have to be standing at the gas pump and start shouting tongues at the top of your lungs. At some times, when it's appropriate, you may feel like you should speak louder; but you can whisper tongues under your breath, and God still hears you. With this in mind you can see that you really could pray in tongues an hour a day or more, even if you are a busy person. And, each time you do, for however long you do, you are body building your spirit, toning it to do the will and purpose God has for you.

Once you start building your spirit; and you are open to the Holy Spirit, you will be amazed at how different things are in your spiritual walk. The voice of God will become clearer to you. When you read the Bible, you will get revelation that you didn't get before. You could read through a spiritual book you have read three times and this time you receive a completely new revelation regarding a topic you did not understand before. The Holy Spirit will also start using you in the other gifts of the Spirit, as he sees appropriate. Something may suddenly come to your mind about someone sitting next to you, that you just know you should share with them, or you should pray with them. You may even find yourself laying hands on someone and they will be supernaturally healed by God's power working through you, or you might see things in the Spirit realm that you have not seen before. As you tone your spirit man by praying in tongues, you may find yourself sitting next to someone on a plane and decide to start praying in tongues, and they will tell you that you were speaking to them in their native tongue, a language that you don't know. This is another type of tongues. Pretty much anything you see supernaturally happening in the Bible, the Spirit can do through you, as He wills, if you are open.

The Bible says in Joel 2:28 referring to the days that many would agree we are living in now, "And it shall come to pass afterward That I will pour out My Spirit on all flesh; Your sons and your daughters shall prophesy, Your old men shall dream dreams, Your young men shall see visions. And also on My menservants and on My maidservants I will pour out my Spirit in those days."

You are the menservants and maidservants that have opened the door. You have accepted the Holy Spirit and you are the sons and daughters that will do these things.

Chapter Three

The Word

Then Jesus said to those Jews who believed Him, "If you abide in My word, you are My disciples indeed. And you shall know the truth, and the truth shall make you free. (John 8: 31-32)

In the previous chapter, I made an analogy of tongues being like exercise for your Spirit. If we exercise our body, we will get stronger, but we will see better results if we eat a well balanced diet. The Word of God or the Bible is the nutrition you need for your Spirit. That makes it another principle to a victorious life with Christ.

The Word of God is a divine, living, breathing book. It contains every promise you will ever need to know from God. It is filled with stories of men and women that were appointed by God and stories about Jesus, God's own son, and how he lived, moved and died on this earth. The Bible says in Psalm 119:105, "Your word is a lamp to my feet And a light to my path." "Your word" in this passage is referring to God's Word and your Bible. Do you have a question about what God would say about your problem? You have His Word available to you every day in your Bible. If you don't know what the Word of God says you are missing out on knowing the basic and important promises God has for you. You will fail to hear and know exactly what He says about how much He loves you and all the things He has done for you.

This is a subject where people are especially prone to excuses about why they can't read the Bible. Have you ever used any of these? "I hunger for the word but I have 3 kids and I just can't make it fit in my day." "It's just not my season, I'm too busy." "I have a two hour commute to work and I am unable to do it, when I'm home I have to spend time with my family." Whatever the excuse, Satan has used it to confuse you and keep you from being as victorious as you were made to be.

Without the Word of God, you cannot have faith; and faith is one of the most fundamental aspects of the Christian walk.

People have many ideas about what the definition of faith includes, and in any dictionary, you will find several definitions. Some use faith to describe your particular religious beliefs. For example, I am of the Christian faith. Others use it to describe belief that something is true without seeing proof beforehand. This is the particular definition I am going to talk about, and it is an important piece. So how do you get faith? Does it just happen when you're born again? Does it happen when you get the baptism of the Holy Spirit? The Bible says in Romans 10:17, "so then faith comes by hearing and hearing by the Word of God." So basically we can say faith comes by hearing the Word of God.

How and where do you hear the Word of God? Well there are many places to hear it. First and foremost, you can hear the Word of God in a good Word preaching church. Everyone should be part of a church congregation, not only to hear the Word, but to get involved with like minded people who will also speak the Word of God to you and your circumstances. You can hear the Word of God by finding a good Bible teacher on the internet. Many churches now have their sermons available for download anytime any place. You can get sermons as a podcast and put them on your MP3 player, or just listen to them on your computer.

There are also several good Bible teachers on TV every single day.

Maybe one of the most important ways to hear the Word of God is to speak it yourself. Mark 11:24 says, "... whatever things you ask when you pray, believe that you receive them, and you will have them". 1 John 5:14,15 says, "...that if we ask anything according to His will, He hears us. And if we know that He hears us, whatever we ask, we know that we have the petitions that we have asked of Him." Don't miss this. If we ask anything that is according to His will, when we pray, and we believe we receive it-it is ours. You won't know what God's will is if you don't know the Word. You won't be able to ask for things and believe with confidence, if you don't know God's promises to you. I'm not just talking about reading the Bible, I'm talking about having it take root in your very being. The Word is like a seed. Jesus talked about this in the parable of the sower we find in Matthew 13. Jesus tells a story of a man sowing seed. Some fell by the wayside and the birds ate it. Some fell on stony ground. It came up quickly but wilted in the hot sun, because it didn't have a root. Some fell in the thorns, and the thorns choked them. Some fell on good ground and yielded a crop. It is important that you hear the Word, and you let it take root in your life.

One of the ways I have found to help the Word to take root is to speak it for your particular situation. The term usually used is confessing it. If you are feeling sick, get into the Word and find out what it says. Find out what the promises are from God in regards to health and wholeness. When you find a verse with a promise about your health, confess it. Jeremiah 30:17 says, "For I will restore health to you And heal you of your wounds, says the Lord..." Recite this verse over out loud, and in your mind. But, don't just confess it. You won't want to forget it. Write the verse down and stick it to your mirror in the bathroom so every time you go in there you remember to say it again. Hang the verse on the inside of your pantry, and every time you open it, you can speak it again. Each time you speak these words, you hear them again which will grow your faith; and faith is believing you receive.

Confessing works both ways, because faith works both ways. If you feel sick and all you do is sit and talk about how sick you are and how horrible you feel and all the negative things you are feeling, you are not believing you receive the promise of divine health from God; so you won't receive it.

Another good way to confess the word is to pray it. Starting in Ephesians 1:17, we see a prayer that Paul was praying for the Ephesians. I pray that prayer, filling in my name or the person I'm praying for at the time. Here is an example of this.

I pray that the God of our Lord Jesus Christ, the Father of glory, May give to (me) the spirit of wisdom and revelation in the knowledge of Him, the eyes of (my) understanding being enlightened; that (I) may know what is the hope of His calling, what are the riches of the glory of His inheritance in the saints, and what is the exceeding greatness of His power toward us who believe according to the working of His mighty power. (Ephesians 1:17-19)

Prayers that Avail Much 25th Anniversary Edition by Germaine Copeland (1997) is an excellent resource for praying and confessing the Word. It is a book that is filled with prayers that have been taken directly from the Word of God, about nearly any situation you or anyone else might experience. This particular edition has several volumes in one book and each has its own set of prayers for different circumstances. A book called The Secret Power of Speaking God's Word by Joyce Meyer (2004) is another excellent resource with several Bible verses for many situations listed in an easy to follow format.

Are you reading the Word of God or do you say things like," I don't have time?" "I have a job and three kids and it's not my season." I am here to tell you that you do not have time not to. The Word of God and the confession of it is what is going to help you be a victorious mother and raise those children healthy and whole and as God would. It is the thing that is going to help you through the work day, help you be a productive worker, and help you to prosper financially; so you can put food on your table and have a roof over your head. It's what's going to help you find peace when you hit that roadblock that you were not expecting, and everything seems to be falling apart. You don't want to decide to start reading and confessing the Word when everything is crazy around you. It takes practice to see things as the Word sees them instead of how the world sees them. It takes practice to look at your checking account, and believe that God will provide, when it says there is $4 in it and you need to buy groceries. Reading and confessing the Word is something you should start doing today. It doesn't have to be an hour long study every day. Start a little at a time. As you keep doing it, chances are you will find time to read and study more.

I have found one of the best places to start reading the Word is to get a good devotional. These are books that have a Bible reading for each day and then usually some teaching on it. It usually will take you about 15 minutes to do a devotional every day. I try to get up before my kids in the morning and do my devotional, because it gives me something to meditate on and pray about during the day. That's right, you have times during the day that you can meditate on the Word. Do you drive in the car? Do you wash dishes on occasion without someone talking to you? You can use those times for God.

I'm not saying it is easy to get up before my kids fifteen minutes every day. It is a tricky endeavor. First of all, I don't like mornings, at all, and they get up early. The last thing I want to do is be up. This may not be the time God would have for you to do this, but ask him and see what you hear. Then do it. I am not perfect, and I struggle with this at times. My alarm goes off in the morning, and my mind is filled with all the excuses of why I should sleep another ten minutes or not get up now at all and just wait for the kids to get me up. Chances are you will have some struggles too whether it would be with this particular point or something else. If you do make time for reading the Word; if you tell your feelings that your spirit is going to win today and you're going to do this no matter how they feel about it, you will be blessed. I know from experience.

Now once you start knowing what the Word says; you start confessing the Word and start believing the Word, it's time to take the next step. That is acting on the Word. It is the next step to letting the Word grow in good soil. The Bible says in James 1:22:

But be doers of the word and not hearers only deceiving yourself. For if anyone is a hearer of the word and not a doer, he is like a man observing his natural face in the mirror; for he observes himself, goes away, and immediately forgets what kind of man he was.

As God gives you an answer from His Word for your situation, take action. Move in the direction He has told you to go.

Are you struggling with something and you don't seem to be getting answers from God? There are several reasons why this might happen. Ask the Holy Spirit to reveal it to you. Did God tell you something to do, and you didn't do it? Did you read in your Word that you were to forgive your neighbor and you had great revelation about it for the moment? Maybe you had the best intentions to call them on the phone, but you forgot. Maybe it wasn't even forgetting; but you got an important call from work you had to take. You got sidetracked and then it was put off for days. When we read the Word and we don't act on it, it can be like in the parable. The seed of the Word that was planted in your heart wilted in the hot sun. Once it's wilted it's easy to forget what it was you we're going to take care of. Like in James 1:22, you forgot what kind of man/or women you were going to be. We all do make mistakes. We are all human. Ask for forgiveness and then do what God has asked you to do as soon as you can. You will probably start seeing things happen spiritually almost immediately.

Now, you're reading the Word of God. You're finding out exactly what God's promises are for your life in every situation. You are receiving great divine revelation from it because you have the Holy Spirit living in you to help bring you to it. You are confessing those promises for your situation and doing what these revelations have told you to do. Because of this, you are believing you receive these promises. You are on your way. Victory is here. "Fight the good fight of Faith…" (1 Timothy 6:12). Is it always easy? Will everything always be perfect now? The Bible says, "…in the world we will have tribulations…" (John 16:33); so it may not always be easy. But this verse goes on to say, "...be of good cheer, for I (Jesus) have overcome the world"; since we are Jesus', if we persevere, we too can overcome anything this world or the evil in it can send our direction.

Chapter 4

The Importance of Worship

Enter into His gates with thanksgiving, And into His courts with praise. Be thankful to Him, and bless His name. For the Lord is good; His mercy is everlasting, And His truth endures to all generations. (Psalm 100: 4-5)

Worship is an integral part of a victorious walk with God. Worship is a chance to meet with God face to face. It is an opportunity to dwell in the presence of the Most High God Himself. It is a time to hang out, and to tell Him how much you love Him. It is a time to be in awe of how great He is and thank Him for the wonderful things He has done for you. It is also

Love God, Live Life

a time to remember He is God, show Him respect and give Him glory.

We have an awesome privilege to be able to actually enter into the presence of God. In the Old Testament, before Jesus died for us on the cross, the presence of God mostly existed behind a wall of many curtains called a veil in a temple. The only people who could enter were very specific people who did very specific sacrifices for their sins. When Jesus died on the cross, He was the perfect sacrifice for us; and we are now able to enter into the presence of God. The Bible says in Matthew 27:51, after describing Jesus' death, that the veil was torn in two. We now have the ability to meet with God face to face; and best of all we can do it in our living room, car or bedroom. It doesn't have to be in a fancy temple and we don't have to shed the blood of an animal to do it.

There are many forms of worship, and many ways to worship. The most important part of worship is your heart. For example, we can worship with our finances by giving tithes and offerings. Giving to God is a form of worship. If we do it out of a wrong heart, however, it's not worship. Worship can be singing in your car to God, singing in your living room, singing at church, or it may not involve singing at all. If you are telling God how much you love Him and how thankful you are to Him, you are worshipping Him. If you are taking time out just for God, just to be with God, you are probably worshipping Him. It's one of the reasons He made you, to hang out with you. He wants to fellowship with you.

The best part of worship is that it is refreshing. If nothing else, it will change your perspective on just about any circumstance because you have decided to stop dwelling on it and start dwelling with God instead. But beyond that, when God feels distant to you, if you worship, He becomes real again. When a problem seems too big, when you worship, it's not just your problem anymore, it's God's. When you're in the midst of a trial, if you take time to Worship, you get refreshed and renewed; and many times you get the answer as well.

How do you worship? Again there is not a formula for this. God does show us patterns in the Word and that's always a good place to start. Mainly He wants your heart. The first and most important thing is to have your heart in the right place. I think the best way to describe it is a reverent heart. God is God. He is all knowing and all powerful, and yet He meets you where you're at. If you are making an effort to worship Him, chances are your heart is in the right place. I said worship didn't need to include music. However, it is a way that many people can and do worship. Many churches start their services with praise and worship music. Why? God likes music, loud music and shouts to Him. So many people say, "I can't worship the Lord, I just can't sing, or I can't play an instrument." It is not important to Him if it sounds good. After all, He made you just the way you are and He knows how it's going to sound if you sing. In Psalm 66:1 the Bible talks about making a joyful noise in some versions. Others say a joyful shout. I think about my 2 year old son. He makes many joyful noises. Most of them are shrieking piercing noises that make your hair stand on end. Yet it makes me smile and sometimes giggle out loud because I know he is so happy. It is the same with our Father God. Even if our "joyful noise" to Him is just noise, He is giggling out loud with us. He is happy.

Worship does not have to be loud, but I am convinced that God likes loud. The Bible has scripture after scripture of loud worshipping—shouting to the Lord, instruments and singing. All through the Old Testament, if the people of Israel were going to show the Lord they were grateful for His goodness and in awe of His glorious works, they shouted. All through Psalms, we see praising with shouting, singing and instruments. It might not be so much about the noise, however. Did you ever notice when you really want to get your point across, you talk louder. Usually that is because you are convinced, and you want to be convincing. If you know that God is good. If you know that God is in control, and God is your healer and provider. If you know what He has done, is doing and that He continues to do great things for you, you are convinced. Your whole heart is in it. You don't have to hold anything back. You are sure. You want Him to know you know. There is a place and time for everything, so it's important to remember that it might not be appropriate for you to start shouting to the Lord in just any and every service you attend; however if you are sensitive to the Holy Spirit, He will guide you. Don't forget, some places, including your bedroom, kitchen or living room, it is absolutely appropriate.

Here is one way to worship. Find some good praise and worship music. Turn it on in your bedroom or your living room and start singing or dancing. If you don't do anything else, just speak the name of Jesus. It takes a little practice for some people to get past their soul, or their feelings. I'm talking about that voice in your head that says, "I feel weird raising my hands, or singing out loud or shouting to God". If you start in a place with only you and God, it helps you get past this. Pretty soon you will see that the Holy Spirit inside of you might prompt you to do certain things, like raise your hands. Something might come to mind to say. Sometimes you will not sing, but you will recite scripture; or you will pray in tongues. Sometimes, you might kneel, sit down or stand up. Sometimes you might just stand still and quiet and bask in God's presence. Some people refer to this quiet worship as soaking. Do what you think you are being moved to do by the Spirit, rather than what you think looks right or what you feel comfortable doing. As you do this more and more you will find yourself getting to a deeper place in your worship with God. You will see what it means to be in the presence of the Most High God. You will truly be able to fellowship with him.

It's important to do this on your own, so when you are in a service with praise and worship you can really praise and worship. It's also important to realize that we can praise and worship anywhere, not just in church; and we should do it at home. After all, God doesn't only show up for us in Church. We should reverence and worship Him just for who He is every day. So many people are afraid to worship with other people, because they may sound bad, or look weird. That's a dangerous thing, and those very thoughts can be brought about by the enemy himself. He wants you to feel self conscience and not enter in because he knows that if you do it's powerful. And if the person next to you enters in, it's even more powerful. If the whole church family does, he doesn't stand a chance.

Worship takes many forms. You don't need to have music to worship, but a lot of times it is the thing that helps us get started or keeps us going when our souls say, "I'm too tired to raise my hands" or "I don't want to look or sound silly to the person next to me". It's at those times that it is important to worship anyway. Just being in a quiet place with a heart that is in awe of God and how good He is can be worship. You can worship the Lord just by starting to recite scripture about how good He is. That's really what most good worship songs are anyway, scripture that is sung. Just say it instead. In Revelations Chapter 4 we see a picture of the throne room where the most Holy God sits. We see how the elders and creatures who are in the presence of God, worship Him. Day and night the creatures say, "...Holy Holy Holy Lord God Almighty, Who was and is and is to come!"(Revelation 4:8) Whenever the creatures give glory and thanks to God, the elders fall down and worship Him as well and say: "You are worthy, O Lord, to receive glory and honor and power; For You created all things, And by Your will they exist and were created."(Revelation 4:11) If you want to be in God's presence, what a better way to do so then to follow the example given in the Bible of those that are in His presence day and night.

Another great way to begin to worship is to sit down and meditate on all the great and wonderful things God has done for you. Sometimes you maybe in a place where it is hard to see the wonderful things God has done. That is the best time to do it. Worshipping God can be the thing that sustains us through trials. It reminds us we are not in control. God is. If you are in a place where it is difficult finding things to be thankful for, start simple. Even things like air, trees and water are things for which to give God praise. Write them down. When your list is ready, take each thing and start praising Him and thanking Him for it. Once you start, your mind will usually start to flow with it more. Just say, "praise God" and speak the name of Jesus. This is a great way to turn your eyes from a bad situation to a good one.

Just as there is a place and time to have loud worship, there is a place and time to bow down. We see all through the Bible that when people worshipped they bowed down. This is an action that shows the highest respect. It is always important to remember God is God, and sometimes we just need to bow down to Him. Sometimes we need to actually physically bow down, and sometimes we need to bow down in our heart.

You can worship if you are busy. You can worship in your room. You can worship washing dishes. You can worship in your car. You can worship while you take a walk and exercise. I like to have some good worship music with me wherever I go. I like to have it on while I'm doing things throughout my day. Sometimes I just stop what I'm doing and raise my hands and say "praise Jesus." Sometimes I sing a song and focus on Him for a few minutes. When you wake up in the morning, worship for a few minutes. You can worship Him while you are in the shower. You can worship Him for a few minutes before bed. He knows your heart and your schedule. He is delighted if you do it for two minutes or two hours. Just do it. Once you do worship for a few minutes, you will want to do it for hours. It is time for us to worship Him because He is good and in control and has the best in mind for us. It is time for us to enter into His presence and meet face to face with our Creator and the Creator of the universe. It's time. Get stirred up in your heart and just start. Start somewhere and the rest will follow.

Chapter 5

Offense and Bitterness – The Victory Blockers

Therefore I say to you, "whatever things you ask for when you pray, believe you receive them and you will have them," "And whenever you stand praying, if you have anything against anyone, forgive him, that your Father in heaven may also forgive your trespasses. But if you do not forgive, neither will your Father in heaven forgive your trespasses." (Mark 11: 24-26)

Offense can be a very dangerous thing in your life. My eyes were really opened to this subject while reading a book called The Bait of Satan by John Bevere (2011). Offense can literally block the victory in your life. It does this by holding you back from the fullness of the plan God has for you. I talked about how the Word of God can be good seed in your life growing into all the promises God has for you in Chapter 3. In contrast, offense can be like a bad seed and if you don't take care of it, it can turn into a bitter root. You will need to remove that bitter root in order to walk victorious in the plan God has for you.

So many people these days are walking around offended. They are offended at what someone said on TV. They are offended at the driver that cut them off at the intersection, or the person who took their parking spot. They are offended by their family, their pastor or their church. We are living in a time when it seems normal to walk around offended. Let me tell you right now, it's not normal. It's not of God, and it's not good for anyone.

First of all, let's just look at it in a purely non-spiritual manner. You drive into a parking lot. You are driving up as someone is leaving their spot. Just as you are about to pull in, someone comes from the other direction and takes your spot without even seeming to notice you. You are angry and offended. It was your spot, and now you have to go find another one. You start murmuring about them under your breath, about how they were raised and then about how awful this whole world has become. Your day has suddenly become unhappy, and you are frustrated. In the meantime, they didn't notice you in the first place, so they didn't know they did anything to offend you. They are in the store happily going about their day, without a care or a second thought about the parking spot. You will never see them again, but your day is more stressed and less happy just because you allowed yourself to get offended. It is not hurting them at all, it's only hurting you.

If you are so easily offended by a stranger in the parking lot, imagine how easy it can be for you to become offended with a family member or someone else you love. It can almost become a bad habit; and the next thing you know, you are offended much of the time. It is a bad trap.

Now let's look at the spiritual implications of this. Offense is the start of not forgiving someone, and not forgiving is the start of bitterness. If you have these in your life, you are probably blocking something good God is planning for you. It's just that simple. I have learned it over and over in my life. If God feels distant to me, I usually need to forgive someone.

It is vitally important that you are free from any offense in your life. That doesn't mean you won't be offended. It means that you will recognize it right away and take care of it. Also, it is vitally important to find any offense that is hidden from past experiences. If you have been offended, it can open a door for evil to work in your life. If you are offended it allows an opening for the enemy to place lies in your mind. These are lies that you may believe about yourself or the person who offended. Sometimes we believe lies for years and we don't even really know we do until our blinders are removed by the truth.

So let's start with the little things. How do we take care of the little day by day things that irritate and offend us. First of all, realize when you have been offended. If you are driving down the road and you suddenly get angry at another driver, you are probably offended. Repent, tell the Lord you are sorry. Most of the time that is enough. It is enough for the Lord anyway. He died on the cross for our sins; and once we repent of them, He doesn't even remember them. The Bible says in Psalm 103:12 that our sins are removed as far as the east is from the west.

Sometimes our soul is stubborn about repenting. Our mind, will, and emotions don't want to repent; or we repent and we still feel hurt or angry. Pray for the person who hurt you and say something like, "I choose to not be offended." Many times, speaking it out loud is enough to help our soul get lined up with our spirit.

Let's face it there are times in our lives when people do genuinely hurt us. Many times, they don't even know they have hurt us, but sometimes they do. Sometimes, they are family members or close friends. Sometimes, they are people that we don't even know, yet we are deeply hurt by their actions or their words. This kind of offense is the hardest type. Usually, it is someone we trusted or love who has hurt us so deep we don't know if we can ever forgive them. This can be desperately difficult, yet it is vitally important to your spiritual life, as well as your physical being, to take care of these things so you can live in the fullness of the blessings God has for you.

God spoke to me through a song and reminded me not to speak lightly about pain. It is real and many times the things that have come against us are unjust. If it was easy to get over some things, and we knew how to do it, we certainly would. This is a place to start to find freedom.

The first step is to decide you want to forgive the person. It is that simple. Your soul may not want to. Your feelings will probably go all over the place, because Satan can work on your feelings. As long as he has you in unforgiveness, he has a foothold in your life. As long as he has you offended, he is able to sneak in and make you believe all sorts of lies, by putting blinders on your eyes and causing many problems for you. Ask Holy Spirit to help you forgive. He is our helper here on earth and our true comforter. Then say out loud that you choose to forgive that person. If your feelings still are not in line with what you're saying, say it again. When you're mind starts telling you things that are contrary to the forgiveness you just gave and spoke say, "I renounce that lie, in Jesus name"; or " I already took care of that and have forgiven that person". This is what faith is—believing that something is true, because we know it is spiritually, even when our feelings are saying otherwise or our eyes are seeing something different.

Next, pray for the person you forgave. Praying for a person who has hurt you can many times be difficult. The Word says in Matthew 5:44 to "...love your enemies, bless those who curse you ...and pray for those who spitefully use you and persecute you." As with all things in the Word, it works. There is something about taking that step that seems to start to get your feelings in line with your spirit.

Finally, ask the Holy Spirit if you are suppose to go to that person and make amends. Many times that will be the way he leads you. At that point make a call, or go and meet the person. A good way to approach that conversation is to ask for forgiveness yourself. You have been offended by something they have done, you have chosen to take offense, so tell them you are sorry for doing so. Sometimes, they will then apologize for their part in it. Sometimes, they will not. That's Okay. You can forgive them anyway. You have done your part and to keep holding on is only hurting you and your spiritual life. Allow God to deal with them.

Sometimes for some reason or another, it is not possible to meet with the person who offended you. It might not be physically safe for you or maybe they are not here with us anymore on this earth. In either of these cases, you could write a letter to them with the same intentions. You don't need to send the letter, unless the Holy Spirit tells you to, but it is healing for your spirit and soul.

There is another type of sneaky offense and unforgiveness. You might not even know you have it. I like to describe this type in pictures. It is offense that started out as a small seed somewhere in your soul, a little something that wasn't all that big. You didn't take care of it, you probably forgot about it and now it has grown into a bitter root. Sometimes it's just a root, but sometimes it's a long winding root with all sorts of little offshoots. Have you ever been gardening and tried to pull one of those kinds of roots out of the soil? Many times you think you have it, but part of it breaks off and then what happens? It grows back. The thing that can make this so detrimental is many times you don't know it's even there. You may know something is there but you don't know exactly what, you just know something is in the way of your victory. Sometimes, you have dealt with it a little bit; but it wasn't completely out so it grew back.

This can be easy to deal with. It just has to be brought to the light so you can see it. Just ask God to reveal to you anyone who you need to forgive. Most of the time a list of names will come to mind. I like to write them down so I can work on them one by one. Sometimes He will not give you a whole list at once but will reveal one person to concentrate on. God knows best how you can accomplish this so He will do what's best for you. Forgive those people and then ask again to make sure you have not missed anyone. As you work on it and you pray for them the root will be pulled out a little at a time. In my case, one day I just knew it was gone. There was such freedom the day I realized the root was completely pulled out.

Once you have the people who you need to forgive, follow the steps I have outlined earlier:

1. Choose to forgive the person and ask Holy Spirit to help you do so.
2. Say out loud that you choose to forgive them.
3. Meet with them, talk to them on the phone, or write a letter, if prompted by the Holy Spirit.
4. Pray for the person.

If you are still struggling emotionally with this process, try to put yourself in their shoes. Attempt to look for something that makes you feel compassion for them.

Don't put this off. There is often a temptation to do this when it's quieter, and you can better hear from God; or when you have time to deal with it. My advice to you is to do it now. Put the book down and get it done if you can. Satan will help you put it off as long as he can with circumstances, noise or any other excuse he can put in your head to not do it. The longer you wait the longer you will be held prisoner. Don't be a prisoner, be set free.

Chapter 6

Prayer and Fasting – A Key to Overcome

❀

So Jesus said to them, "Because of your unbelief; for assuredly, I say to you, if you have faith as a mustard seed, you will say to this mountain, 'Move from here to there,' and it will move; and nothing will be impossible for you. However, this kind does not go out except by prayer and fasting." (Matthew 17: 20-21)

Prayer is very important to a victorious walk with God. Each and every principle I have outlined involves prayer. There are many types of prayer, but they all involve talking to God. If you have a relationship with a person, you talk to them.

Love God, Live Life

Sometimes it's a close relationship and you talk to them every day. Sometimes you need to make special time to talk to them. You can talk to God whenever you want about whatever you want day and night. He answers prayers.

Have you ever prayed and prayed and not felt like you received an answer? You know what your asking is the will of God for your life, because it is in the Word. You're confessing verses in the Bible that describe exactly what you need, and you just don't seem to get your breakthrough. We don't know the mind of God and some things we will not know until we meet Him in heaven. Yet, one reason you may not be getting an answer may be that you have a subtle unbelief or doubt at work in you. How do you overcome that unbelief? One answer is fasting.

At the end of Matthew Chapter 17, we see that Jesus' disciples had attempted to cast out a demon in a boy and were unable to do it, so the boy wasn't healed. When Jesus came He rebuked the demon in the boy, and he was healed from that moment on. The disciples were confused, so they asked Jesus later why they were not able to cast out the demon. Jesus had a couple of answers. First, He said in verse 20 that it was because of their unbelief. He tells them if they have the faith of a mustard seed, they can move mountains. Then in verse 21, He says, "this kind does not go out without prayer and fasting." For years, I thought this meant that some mountains will just not move no matter how much faith we have if we don't fast. I also thought it meant specifically for demonic deliverance. Now, thanks to some teaching by Dave Roberson, and his book The Walk of the Spirit The Walk of Power (1999) I have new understanding of this exchange between Jesus and his disciples. First of all, I do believe that Jesus was talking about demonic deliverance, because that was the situation he was dealing with. Many times the mountains we are dealing with are related to and in need of demonic deliverance. But now, I also understand that what He is saying is that it is not actually the demon that is moved from the fasting but rather our unbelief. You see if we have true perfect faith there is not room for unbelief. A mustard seed is a very tiny seed. We only need a tiny amount of true faith to move a mountain, but if we have only a tiny amount of unbelief, that mountain won't move.

So you say, I really do believe. I know I believe. There is not an ounce of unbelief in me. I know how you feel. I have been there myself. I have cried out to God with every ounce of everything in me and thought there is not room for unbelief, and, my victory does not come. Now, God does have his own timing, and God does know more than us. His infinite plan for our lives is far above and beyond anything we can comprehend. Sometimes He answers and we miss it because we are looking for something specific and His answer is not what we expected. But, when it comes to sickness for example, it is never God's will for you to be sick. It is just out of the realm of possibility. If we go through the Word of God, Jesus didn't leave people sick. The Word says about Jesus in 1 Peter 2:24, "who Himself (Jesus) bore our sins in His own body on the tree, that we, having died to sins, might live for righteousness-by whose stripes you were healed." This means that Christ not only died for your sins but for our health. The Word talks about covenant blessings with God in Deuteronomy 7. If you keep the law, you will not be cursed to be sick. Keeping the law means you do not sin. Since Christ died on the Cross, we, as born again believers, have the covenant with God, because He is our perfect sacrifice. He covered our sins with His blood, so we are not under the curse of the law anymore but the blessings. The mistaken idea that God has put sickness on you to teach you something is a lie from Satan himself. So, you don't have to have any doubt in this area. Rebuke that sickness and believe that it is gone and it is. Then receive the gift of healing God has already given you.

Now that is easy to say right? What happens if I still feel sick, yet I really do feel like I believe I am healed. There are many possibilities as often there are with God. That doesn't mean it's not His will for you to be well. One possibility might be that there is subtle unbelief in our flesh that is hidden, and you probably don't know it exists. I have mentioned before that we are a three part being. We are spirit, soul and body. Our body is where our sickness lies, but our soul can make us feel like we are sick and that can derail our belief. One answer to exposing this subtle unbelief and removing it from our lives is fasting.

Because our body is reliant on things in this world, and our soul is reliant on our body, one way to shut the body and soul down completely and know that your spirit is in a position of control, at least for the moment, is to deprive them of something they seem to need. Shutting down the flesh puts our spirit first. To shut down the flesh is to shut out every possibility of influence that Satan or his cohorts can have on us as believers. That deprivation can be done by fasting. There are many types of fasting. You can fast all food or a certain type of food, like sweets or coffee or soda. You can fast from your computer or video games or

TV. The best way is to ask God to show you exactly what you should fast. You can ask Him how long to fast as well. Many times that can be up to you.

One of the fasts that God has shown me in my life is a brown rice and juice fast. I will eat nothing but brown rice, juice, and water for usually a period of 3 days. In that time, I do as the Word says in Matthew 6:17, "But you, when you fast, anoint your head and wash your face". Jesus goes on to say in verse 18 that you shouldn't look to others like you are fasting. I take this in modern times to mean, to take a shower and clean up. As I'm fasting, and taking care of the responsibilities of mom and wife, I am in a state of constant prayer. At least as much as I can be on mommy duty. I pray while in the shower, washing dishes and in the car. I ask God for a breakthrough in a particular area, before I start the fast, and then I don't ask God again. I thank God that it is already done in Jesus name, and then say that I receive the answer. I also do a lot of praying in tongues when I'm fasting. What better way to be sure that circumstances are lining up with God's will for my life, but to pray out His perfect plan for it in tongues? I will fast until I believe God tells me to stop. Many times, I will ask Him if I am where I need to be or if I'm released from this fast. Sometimes He will answer and say that it is truly up to me to fast. I can start and stop whenever I want to stop; but if I'm going to get to the breakthrough I need, I should keep going. Sometimes He tells me to feast. Those are the words I usually receive when I know that I am done with a fast, "You can feast."

I have never regretted fasting. I have always received some breakthrough when I have fasted. It may not always be the exact breakthrough that I thought I needed or wanted, but it's a breakthrough. It's interesting though, that even if it's not the breakthrough I thought I needed or wanted it is more perfect, because it was God's plan.

When you are fasting, you will probably feel weak. Satan uses that to get you to stop. Satan will put roadblocks in the way of anything you do to get closer to God, closer to your victory; and to get more revelation in your life. He wants you to live in defeat all of the time. He knows that the more you put your spirit in control, the less control he has. It is important to be aware of this. Don't let it be a reason not to move forward. The Bible says, "But He said to me, "My grace is sufficient for you, for My power is made perfect in weakness."(2 Corinthians 12:9 ESV). That is a promise that if you are seeking God and He feels far away or like He is not in your circumstances, keep on seeking because He is actually strong, and you are probably on the edge of breakthrough.

So are you ready to get closer to your breakthrough? Are you ready to see answered prayer in your life? Are you ready to move closer to a place of peace in the Lord that you are now missing? Then fast today. Ask God to show you what to fast, how long to fast, and dedicate it to Him.

Chapter 7

Spiritual Warfare

Yet in all these things we are more than conquerors through Him who loved us. For I am persuaded that neither death nor life, nor angels nor principalities nor powers, nor things present nor things to come, nor height nor depth nor any other created thing shall be able to separate us from the love of God which is in Christ Jesus our Lord. (Romans 8:37-39)

Entire books have been written on spiritual warfare, and it is a huge in-depth subject that you could study for years. Yet, it is an incredibly important subject in order to live a victorious life for Christ. It is desperately important to understand that there is a spirit realm, how it works, and the authority you have because of Christ in you. This is because Christ died on the cross for you, and you have asked Him to be your Savior when you became born again. It is also important to realize the power that you have which dwells inside your spirit. The Holy Spirit, who raised Jesus from the dead, lives and works inside you when you are baptized in the Spirit. With His power and authority and a little understanding, you have the ability to overcome any attack the devil may bring against you.

Each and every step in this book is a powerful move closer to your Lord and Savior Jesus and a more victorious life in Him. Each and every step in this book is also a step that Satan does not want you to take, because he does not want you to have victory. The last thing he wants for you to know and understand is your standing with Christ; the power available to you through the Holy Spirit, the power of the living and breathing Word of God available to you each and every day; and the trap of unforgiveness and unbelief. He would much rather you stay in your state of powerlessness, defeat and ignorance. He would much rather keep you too busy to take any steps towards victory with Christ. He wants to lie, steal and cheat you into believing you are something you're not. Satan would prefer you not be able to come to a place where your spirit man rules, rather than your flesh; so he is still able to move in your life. For this reason, he will do everything in his power, which is not as powerful as that which is in you, to keep you from taking any of the steps in this book.

Right now you may be thinking it may not be worth it to move forward, because with every step you take, it seems as though things you are stuggling with get more challenging. They don't appear to be turning around anytime soon. It might seem that way at least for awhile. Well, let me tell you right now, that is Satan trying to deter you. It is worth it. It is vital that you push through. You can and will come out victorious if you do.

The key is not running and hiding from Satan and his tactics but to understand how to deal with them when they come against you. The key is knowing that they will come against you and moving forward regardless. The key is not allowing him to win but standing on the promise in Romans 8:28 that "...all things work together for good for those who are called according to his purpose." You are the one who is called according to his purpose, if you are born again.

Let us outline how Satan may come against you and some of ways to work against them. The way he comes against us the most often is in our thoughts. He will put thoughts in your mind to distract you or derail you. They often come with doubt about some breakthrough you have had, and if you believe them he wins. For example, you have prayed to receive the baptism of the Holy Spirit. You ask God to give you evidence of it by speaking in other tongues. You open your mouth and something comes out that is not English. At first, you may be excited and believe, but almost inevitably the thought will come to your mind that it's not really tongues, your just making it up on your own. That's Satan trying to derail you with thoughts. Don't believe them. Here's another example: You pray the prayer of Salvation, and you are excited to get to know your Savior. You are so thankful that He died on the cross for your sins, and you are going to heaven. Then the thought comes that it is not true. You are not going to heaven. Is there even a heaven? This is Satan working in your thoughts. Don't believe it. One of the tactics I have learned to deal with thoughts like this is to say, "I renounce that lie in Jesus name." Then I try to reflect on the truth which is in the Word of God. I ask Holy Spirit to remind me, "What is the truth?" At this point, the truth will most likely just be there in your thoughts to ponder and believe instead of the lie.

Love God, Live Life

Another way Satan will come against you is in your circumstances. He will line up circumstances to make it look like you have not had the victory you have been waiting for. Many times, it even happens after you have received the victory, and you know it. He will put people or things in your path that make you believe something different than you know. Here is an example of this: You are believing for a financial miracle. You read through the Word and realize that tithing is an important piece to financial victory. You pray and believe. You even fast, believing God will come through with a financial blessing. You plan your budget, removing things that are not important, so you can get to a place that you can tithe. Then you do it, you write out your first check. It all looks great, and your car breaks down and you have an unexpected repair expense. Satan has thrown something in the way of tithing, because he knows that is the way for you to receive the blessing. Do you stop? Or, do you keep tithing, believing God will provide for you. The finances start flowing, and you finally pay off your last medical bill. You're praising God for all his greatness. Then your four year old climbs up on the bunk bed, falls off, hurts her arm and needs to go to the emergency room. Now you have another medical bill to pay. Satan has put a circumstance in your way to derail you. Don't let him.

This is a very real and easy way for him to work in the lives of people here on this earth, because people have free will, and many of them don't follow and obey the voice of God. Even those who do follow and obey God's voice, can miss it sometimes. How do you deal with Satan's tactics? The best way is not to let it derail you. The less it derails you the less Satan will bring that particular thing against you, because he knows it doesn't work.

I also believe it is very important to be pro-active with your spiritual warfare. What does that mean? It means you have been given the authority to use the name of Jesus, and The Word says all things must bow to the name of Jesus. Phillipians 2:10,11 says, "that at the name of Jesus every knee should bow, of those in heaven, and of those on earth, and of those under the earth, and that every tongue should confess that Jesus Christ is Lord, to the glory of God the Father." It means you, since you have Christ in you and are made in the image of Christ, can rebuke the devil and all his powers. It means that you have the authority to plead the blood of Jesus. Not only do you have the authority to do so, you have the responsibility. Doing so can provide protection in this world to anything you put under the blood of Jesus. Declaring something covered in the Blood of Jesus will cause anything that is not of God to flee.

Let's look at some practical ways that you can do this everyday in your life. First thing in the morning, you might pray something like the following prayer.

> Evil, I cancel your assignment in the name of Jesus on (Name), (Name), my finances, my health, and all my Father God has given me in this life. Father God, I cover (each person), my finances and all you have given me in this life with the blood of Jesus. Angels, I appoint you in the name of Jesus to surround and protect these people and things today.

I received revelation one time that the blood of Jesus is powerful, and pleading the blood over things is very important. God also showed me that covering in the blood can be even more effective. It is also effective to rebuke demons in Jesus' name, tell them to leave. Say they are under your feet. Tell them their place is not with you. And, it is effective to use The Word as well. One verse I use is "No weapon formed against you shall prosper..." (Isaiah 54:17) There are many scripture references and prayers written from scripture references that are useful for spiritual warfare. A good book for this is, Prayers that Avail Much 25th Anniversary Edition by Germaine Copland (1997). This book has 3 books in one and has many great prayers for this purpose.

Once you are taking steps to be proactive, it's important to take care of anything that you need to spiritually. The Lord gave me revelation once that some things I could just rebuke, and they would go; but some things I had to let out. These things may be habits that need to be taken care of because they open doors to allow evil to work. Examples of these things may be addictions, fears, bitterness, watching or listening to inappropriate things, or not being obedient in something that God has asked of us. Ask the Holy Spirit. He will show you if there are any doors standing open to allow evil to work in your life. Tell the evil to leave in Jesus name and ask the Holy Spirit to help you close the doors. If it doesn't seem like a door is closing you probably need to forgive someone. It is really that easy.

Spiritual warfare on behalf of other people can fall in the somewhat challenging realm. The Word says in Ephesians 6:12, "For we do not wrestle against flesh and blood, but against principalities, against powers, against the rulers of the darkness of this age, against spiritual hosts of wickedness in the heavenly places." That means we are not fighting against people, we are fighting against darkness. People have free will. That free will, mixed with a lack of understanding or blindness caused by the lies of Satan; can cause difficulties in relationships and circumstances while we are here on this imperfect earth. You can rebuke those spirits and they will go. Keep in mind, however, that we all have free will. You have no control over what others decide to do in their lives. Each person has the free will to open or close doors to evil. All you can do is pray for them.

Once you understand a few of these easy steps, spiritual warfare becomes actually rather simple. Every single principle I have outlined in this book can be undermined if you don't know a little about spiritual warfare. If you understand the basics, you can recognize when the power of darkness comes against you. Then you can take steps to move forward, rather than being sidetracked or thrown off course. Believe the truth and renounce the lies. Then move forward into victory.

Chapter 8

Putting It Together – A Victorious Life

W hat does a victorious life with Christ look like? Is it the same for everyone? How do you know if you have reached it? How do you know that you are really putting God first? How can you be sure that you are not making something more important in your life than God? We live in a world where these questions are common. We also live in a world that is distracting in many ways. Anything Satan can use to distract us from our calling, he will use. Anything he can sneakily put in the way of victory, he will put in the way. Any lie Satan can make us believe to keep us from fullness with Christ he will use. Let's face it, there are so many distractions in this world sometimes Satan doesn't have to have anything to do with it. So, what is a person to do? I have outlined seven principles in this book. They are by no means the only ones. I've said before, I don't believe there is a specific formula for everyone. Only God knows what each and every person needs. But, if you follow these principles, you will be able to find yourself in a place where you can have a personal relationship with the Lord of the universe, hear His voice, and find the plan He has for your life.

Often I hear the excuse, "I'm just too busy, God understands, it's just not my season of life to do these things." It is true that there is a season for all things. The word is clear on this. Just be careful. Do not use this as an excuse to do nothing. Sometimes we don't even know that's what we are doing. Satan is great at distorting the truth just a little to make you believe a lie. If you have a relationship with your Lord and Savior, you can avoid many of the traps of Satan that get in your way. You can learn to hear the voice of God and ask him what He would have you do next, instead of guessing and moving forward by your own power. You can learn to walk in the blessings God has for you, such as divine health and prosperity, instead of being moved day to day by sickness, or lack. You can know the power that is in you and pray in tongues, praying out the perfect plan for your life with a language that evil cannot understand nor come against. As you pray that perfect plan, you will strengthen your Spirit to a place where you can overcome the things of your flesh that hold you back. You can come to a place in the Spirit where you clearly recognize the voice of God and know each of the steps you should take to move forward. Just think, you can get to a place where your circumstances can change, your flesh can change, and that will change everything else.

I am a busy wife and mother of 3 and I would have never thought that I had enough time in my life to do anything victorious for God, much less write a book on the subject. I was hungry and I would read a book about the subject and then the lies would come from Satan. "Cool, praying in tongues is so great for your spirit man but you don't have time to pray in tongues for 3 hours a day." The truth is, any time you spend praying tongues is better than none. I would get excited about reading the Word and reciting it; and then the lie would come, "You won't get anything out of that unless you put some real time into it....you don't have that kind of time." The truth is, that any amount of time you spend in the Word is better than none. And, if you have the power of the Holy Spirit behind it, the ten minutes you do spend, can make more difference in you than the three hours someone spent without the revelation power of Him. It is important to know that if you do your part, God will do the rest.

If you repent and ask to be born again, the Holy Spirit will do the rest. If you start to pray in tongues, the Holy Spirit will put God's perfect prayer for your life in you and pray it through your spirit. If you open The Word with the power of the Holy Spirit living inside you, He will bring the revelation. If you go even further and decide to meditate on that Word throughout your day, He will grow that seed into something you would have never even imagined.

If you take the time to raise your hands in praise for ten minutes with a heart of true worship, He will meet you at that place; and chances are you won't want to quit, even when it's time to move forward with your day. If you take the time to take care of your unforgiveness and bitterness, and take steps to move past it, the Lord God will remove the bars that have had you imprisoned, and you will find freedom. If you take a day or two to fast, you may not believe the breakthrough you reach, and how the Spirit will change you and your circumstances. Finally, if you learn a few basics of spiritual warfare, nothing can hold you back. None of it takes a lot of time. Mostly, it's just starting. You do your part and God does the rest.

So how does a day really look for a busy person who is going to follow these principles to follow our Lord and Savior. First, pray the prayer and become born again. That's easy. It's fast and once you have done it, it is done. Next, become baptized with Holy Spirit. This can happen right after you are born again, or right now if you have been born again and never been baptized in the Spirit. Just invite the Holy Spirit to make a home in your spirit. Then ask to have evidence with tongues. Open your mouth and speak them out. It is a gift that has already been given to us on the day of Pentecost so all you really have to do is receive the gift. It really can be that easy. And once it is done it is done, you don't have to do it again. Unfortunately, many people have hindrances to tongues, and it might not happen just like this, but it can. Ask the Holy Spirit to help you get past your mind, will and emotions. Fast if you have to fast. Ask somebody to pray with you. Don't get too hung up on it. Sometimes, that is the problem. If the tongues don't happen right away, continue to believe you received it, and move on. They can and will come.

If you have children, try to wake up in the morning a little bit before them. If you don't have children, get up a little earlier

Love God, Live Life

than normal. This may be difficult for you, remember Satan doesn't want you to succeed at this, and your flesh isn't used to being obedient to your spirit. Do it anyway. If you don't get up one day, don't get hung up on it, just try again the next day. Ask the Holy Spirit to wake you up when you need to wake up. When you get up, start with spiritual warfare. Start by canceling assignments for evil on you, your family, and everyone God has given you in this life. Then, cover each of these people in the blood of Jesus, by saying just that, "Father, I cover (name) in the blood of Jesus." You can use prayers from one of the books I have suggested to do this. Now, do something with The Word. I like to use a devotional. It's amazing how God will speak to you through this daily time with Him. Once you have The Word from your particular devotional, keep it in your mind. Ask the Holy Spirit to give you revelation related to it during the day. You may want to write it down on a post-it note and stick it in your lunch to remind you when you arrive at work, or if you stay at home put it someplace in your home. Now, you have spent about 15 minutes extra in your day, and you have spent time with God. You have done some, and he will do the rest. At this point, if you need to get in the shower or get ready to go to work, pray in tongues in the shower, while you're making breakfast, or while you're driving. You can also put some worship music on in your home while you are getting ready, or in your car. I like to have worship music going throughout the day, as I go about my motherly duties. At some point, I usually will just stop and raise my hands in worship here and there. What a great way to prepare for your day, to worship on your commute or pray out God's perfect plan for you while you're getting ready or in rush hour.

As you go about your day, have an open conversation with the Lord about everything that happens, big and little. This will help you learn to distinguish his voice. It's good to practice with the little things, so that when the big things happen, you will know how to hear Him. At any point and time, you can hear three voices. One, the voice of your mind. One, the voice of evil, and one the voice of God. The voice of your mind will often sound like emotion, this is not the voice of God. The voice of evil will often sound right but if you really examine it, it will not line up with the word of God. The voice of God, always lines up with the Word. This is why it is important to practice. If you don't feel like you hear the voice of God, which many people feel like they don't, renounce the lie in Jesus name. The truth is in the Word. In John 10:4,5 we read,

"And when he brings out his own sheep, he goes before them; and the sheep follow him, for they know his voice. Yet, they will by no means follow a stranger, but will flee from him, for they do not know the voice of strangers." The passage goes on to describe Jesus as the good shepherd. The truth is, if you are seeking the voice of God, you will hear the voice of God. It takes a little practice. Don't be afraid to follow because even if you mess up you have the promise in Romans 8 that all things work together for good. Believe it and follow. Pray in tongues. As your spirit man is edified, it will become more apparent when you hear the voice of God and when you hear another voice. Your inner witness, the Holy Spirit watches out for you. Trust Him and believe.

Find a few quiet moments and ask the Lord to tell you if you are holding any bitterness or unforgivness. Ask Him to tell you names of anyone you should forgive and listen. You may be surprised who comes up. Once you have the names, forgive them. Follow the steps outlined in Chapter 5. God may give you these names in stages. You may forgive several people and then ask again and find out that you have more. You may forgive someone and then find yourself falling back into unforgiveness. Keep up on this. Ask Holy Spirit to show you when something happens. Then can take care of it immediately, instead of holding on to it for years and forgetting it even has you held captive.

When things are difficult, worship. When you need a pick me up, worship. When things are going great, worship. Thank God for the blessings he has given. When you need a specific answer, seek God first, instead of reasoning through it in your mind for hours or days. This takes practice. Start somewhere, and God will do the rest.

When you hit an impasse, consider fasting for a time. Ask Holy Spirit to show you how to effectively fast while you are going about your daily duties. Maybe it is fasting a meal and going to your car and praying instead. Maybe it's giving something up that takes up time and pray. Maybe it's a brown rice and juice fast for a period of time. Ask, and God will reveal it to you. When you hear, listen and do what you heard.

This is just one example of how a busy person may go about following these principles. In this example, you have only really taken a few extra minutes of your morning. The rest you do in between your normal duties. It is really more about being open to trying and reminding yourself to do these things when you are able. As you start, you will become hungrier, and as you become hungrier, it will be easier to find the time;

because pretty soon other things that were important to you before will seem less important.

Whenever possible, spend some specific quiet time with the Lord. Here is something you can try. Lock yourself in your room with worship music and do as the Spirit leads you to do. Sometimes you will just sit quiet and listen. Sometimes you will dance. There is nothing quite as refreshing. There is little that will change your outlook on anything more than quiet time with God or worship from the heart.

This is how I fit these principles into my busy life. It may be different for you. You may do it in a different order. If you ask the Holy Spirit to guide you, He will. Do not get hung up on specifics to the point that you don't do anything. That is such a trap. If this happens, just start over the next day. The Bible says in Romans 8:1, "There is therefore now no condemnation to those who are in Christ Jesus, who do not walk according to the flesh, but according to the Spirit." That means you never have to feel guilty and quit. You can repent and start over. If you repent, your Father will not even remember where you have fallen short, He will only rejoice in the progress you have made.

Now you have the tools to get started. Get hungry, and when you do, there is no telling where God will lead you. He has a plan and purpose for your life. It can be easy to find it. Once you've found it, it's amazing what God will do daily in your life. Take a step, do something, and God will do the rest.

Bibliography

Bevere, John (2011). *The Bait of Satan: Living Free from the Deadly Trap of Offense.* Lake Mary, Florida: Charisma House

Copeland, Germaine (1997). *Prayers that avail much.* Tulsa Oklahoma: Harrison House Inc.

Meyer Joyce (2004) *The Secret Power of Speaking God's Word.* New York, New York: Faith Works.

Roberson, Dave (1999) *The Walk of the SPIRIT; The Walk of POWER: The Vital Role of Praying in Tongues.* Tulsa Oklahoma: Dave Roberson Ministries